CW00369441

Working things out

Tracy Reynolds

 Strategic Book Publishing

Copyright © 2009
All rights reserved – Helen Tracy Reynolds

No part of this book may be reproduced or transmitted in
any form or by any means, graphic, electronic, or mechanical,
including photocopying, recording, taping, or by any infor-
mation storage retrieval system, without the permission,
in writing, from the publisher.

Strategic Book Publishing
An imprint of Strategic Book Group
P. O. Box 333
Durham, CT 06422
www.StrategicBookGroup.com

ISBN: 978-1-60860-300-8

Printed in the United States of America

Interior Book Design: Judy Maenle

Dedication

*To all those who have encouraged me
to follow my calling and to
Shaeron Caton-Rose for
her beautiful illustrations*

Contents

Working things out

Miscellaneous

The adolescent says...

I saw you looking at me last night
and I wondered did you know
the way that I was feeling
as you stared across the room?

I saw you looking at me last night
and I wondered did you know
the confusion I was feeling
as I blushed and turned aside?

I saw you looking at me last night
and I wondered did you know
that I looked at you as you turned away
and wished you'd turn around?

Night draws in.

Soft swathes of cloud
caress the hillsides,
drawing deep purple brush strokes
over the grass.

Blood-red fingers of sunlight,
dipped in blue-black ink
sink gracefully into oblivion.

A single bird protests
at the coming night
as all sinks into darkness
and deep slumber.

What about me?

It's hard to be what other people want,
to fulfil expectations which are not your own.
It's hard to define them, you see,
like climbing a mountain you didn't want to
on someone else's behalf.

Are there?

Are there places you never return from,
steps once taken,
that cannot be retraced?

Is it possible that some things
once done
cannot be undone?

Are some things unforgivable?
Actions which are
carved into eternity?

Is it possible that some things
are just meant to be?

Linear beings

It's always struck me as odd that
as I can only move forward in time,
I should spend so much of it looking back.
Will tomorrow be the same as yesterday?
If only?

And although I'm only here
in this moment in time,
I worry so much about the future.
Will tomorrow be the same as today?
What if?

What if I could be satisfied
with living this moment—now?
Would I be happier?
Will today be all I hope for?
Who knows?

Why is life so complicated?

Wanted to write something philosophical
and full of worldly wisdom.
Wanted to be concise, full of smart replies
and witty epitaphs.
Wanted to write something unique
and stunning in its simplicity.
Wanted to write reams of
knowledgeable somethings
that only the elite would understand.
Wanted to say something fantastic, brilliant,
and of its time.
Wanted to be the only one who
grasped the essence of the problem
in a nutshell.
Why is life so complicated?
God knows!

The morning

Deep, glittering, crystal waves
of light gently lapping the
dew-adorned grass.

Orange-bright reflections
sparkle in sunlit windows
as dawn breaks.

Limbs stretch and voices sprawl
over the peaceful landscape.
Breakfast is ready.

Hurricanes of blue and grey,
laced with glowing faces,
whirl downstairs.

Clattering cutlery and energetic
exclamations fill the air
across the breakfast table.

Whirlwinds of exercise books
and backpacks stumble out
into the day.

The tones of hastily slammed door
reverberates around the house,
echoes in the hall.

Then peace descends to heal the wounds
of noise, and rush, and haste.
Another day begins.

Difficult questions

It's funny, isn't it,
how He came
to accept the unacceptable,
comfort the inconsolable,
heal the incurable,
dispossess the powerful?

It's funny, isn't it,
how we try
to align ourselves with the respectable,
avoiding the pain of others,
deepening the hurts we bear,
to court the powerful?

It's funny, isn't it,
that He chose
to ask the difficult question,
reveal the hidden agenda,
love the unlovable
to death and destruction?

It's funny, isn't it,
how we choose
to avoid the tougher issues,
keep secret our deepest needs,
and ignore the unattractive
in search of life and happiness?

The Canaanite woman

The trouble with God is that He won't be
contained,
restricted,
denied access,
follow the rules,
stay inside.
God breaks out, refuses to live in a box,
declines our polite invitation to stay in His seat,
sends His regrets that He will not be attending our services.
The trouble with God is that we find Him on the outside,
living with the outcast,
sleeping rough, no shoes on His feet.
The trouble with God is that He loves the unlovable,
unconditionally, despite everything, still loves.

Sometime in the future an angry and desperate woman
    is following a group of men.
"Just like a woman to cause trouble!"
"Just like a foreigner to go where she shouldn't!"
"Just like her sort not to know when enough is enough!"
"Just like her not to understand that she is insignificant!"
Invisible!
Powerless!
A nameless woman!
A nothing!
A less-than-nothing!
She trudges through the streets, pushes her way
    through the crowds, following and shouting,
    shouting and following.
Why does nobody listen?
Why does nobody care?
She has tried everything! Paid doctors, bought potions.
Until . . . she hears about this Man. She knows this Man
    can help. She's heard He is from God. She knows about
    God—doesn't know how she knows, but she does.

He speaks to her heart—a voice calling her name.
    She wants to know who He is
and so, she dares to do what she shouldn't—she approaches
    the Man in the street.

The other women, the respectable women, the women
    who know their place,
whisper to each other,
"Where is her husband?"
"Why doesn't he stop her?"
"Making a spectacle of herself!"

"Isn't she the one with the daughter?"
"Yes, yes – no wonder with a mother like that . . . !"
"She's not one of us!"
"She has no right to approach Him!"
"She shouldn't be here!"
"Out in the street!"
"Shouting!"
"Following!"
"Shouting and following!"
"She has no right . . . !"

But in her desperation, her desperation and love
    for her child, her daughter,
she follows.
Anger drives her. Desperation pushes her on.
I will see Him!
I will make Him listen to me!

He will not walk away!
I will not be left behind!
Now is the time!
Now is my time!

And then she sees Him, walking the streets, God in Man;
    and she cannot let Him pass.
She will have her answer!
He will not turn away from her!
She will speak to Him for her child,
her beloved; she *will* speak!

The men around Him are jeering, embarrassed by
    her persistence,
appalled by her boldness.
"Who does she think she is?"
"She doesn't belong!"
"Now is *our* time!"
"We are the chosen!"
"We are the ones to whom God speaks!"
"We are the ones He walks with!"
"We protect Him from the outsiders,
keep Him safe in our midst."
"We cannot allow Him to be touched!"
"Tainted!"
"Spoiled!"
"Stained by the outcast!"
"Send her away . . . !"
"Tell her to get lost . . . !"

She is already lost. Lost and alone.
Outsider!
Outcast!
What is left to lose?

Still she follows and shouts, shouts and follows.
    Refuses to give up.
Will not be left behind. Finally she stands in front of them,
    eyes flashing,
hands on hips; she will not be denied her moment.

The men around Him look at her; their eyes show—*what?*
    Amusement!
What? Is this a joke to them? Is this funny to them?

She clenches her teeth. Her anger boils. She turns to
    the God / Man,
in expectation. And He is diffident, unwilling even,
    to acknowledge her right.

She will not be moved. She has come too far.
    A few bread crumbs,
that's all she wanted. Not much—is it? A few bread crumbs,
    not much to ask.
A few bits of the leftovers, those few crumbs that will be
    shaken off the cloth,
swept onto the floor, fed to the dogs. Not much to ask.

Then the swift exchange of a few words. A seemingly
    insignificant conversation.
A few words of challenge—defiance even?

A few words, not many. Just a few—
a short banter,
a battle of wits,
a crossing of verbal swords.
Over a few bread crumbs.
Why?

For a few breadcrumbs? The bits that no one wants?
    The bits that no one notices,
like her.?
Insignificant!
Unseen!
Discarded!
But to Him,
Precious.

Important enough to argue over. Significant enough not
    to just give away.
And she will not be denied.

And He is surprised by her response, delighted by her wit,
    amazed by her faith,
as she stands there waiting for her answer.

This outcast, this invisible, this forgotten breadcrumb,
    is faithful, is precious,
is loved.
Belongs to Him.

The rich young man

You always want more! No matter what I give,
    You always want more!
I have followed.
I have listened.
I have given,
and yet You still demand, like an angry toddler,
    screaming in dismay!

Can I help where I was born?
Can I help that I have been wise, and invested well?
And my reward from You? Another demand!
You say, "Give it all away." And if I do, who will
    support You?
People like me make it possible for people like YOU
    to do what YOU do!

And you! You act as judge and jury! You assume I will
    not give it up!
How do you know that? How many of you would do
    the same?
How many of you do?
How do you know that in time
I didn't grow to understand? To give it all away?
    Or, perhaps,
understanding exactly the implications of His request,
    declined His offer of freedom
and sought to buy myself some peace instead?

Christmas

The beginning

It was the beginning of beginnings.
When God created.
When God initiated.
When God invented.

It was in the beginning when God arose, and formed
    the Word,
and breathed the Word of life.

It was the beginning of life and the beginning of words.

God breathed the beginning words and a world was born.
    God spoke and the words became—light and dark,
    animals and plants, sea and land, and people.

It was the beginning of the God breathed timeless words
    of love; of the relationship of love, of God loving the
    world he had made, of the created loving their creator.

God adopted and embraced, established and founded.

It was the beginning of speaking, of words, of communication.
It was the beginning of apples and serpents.
It was the beginning of people.
Of imagination and creativity.
Of potential and authenticity.
Of truth and grace.
Of knowing love and acceptance.
Of human loving and creating.
Of passing on the words of love from God.

It was the beginning of God and the creation forever
    intertwined.

And that was the end of the beginning and the beginning
    of becoming.
And with the becoming came the beginning of choice,
    of freedom, of independence,
of the potential for wrongdoing and exploitation.
For misleading and being misled,
for corruption and perversion,
for evil and wickedness.

And it became the beginning of bad choices,
of death and murder, of hurt and heartache.
Of struggling to hear God's words of love, of losing the way,
of forgetting the beginning and the God who began
    everything.

It was the beginning of the end—
The end of life.
The end of relationship.
The end of light.
But it was not the end of love.

God breathed the timeless words of love in the beginning
    and they echoed down the centuries, whispered through
    time, inspired the imagination of those who caught
    the sound, and continued to speak the words of the
    beginning.
And those words of love encouraged the brokenhearted,
    strengthened the weak,
comforted the mourning, reassured the poor.

Down the centuries the beginning words of love provoked
    and animated the prophets,
heartened and invigorated the leaders of Israel, fortified and
    stimulated the people of God.
Until the time of the new beginning.

The beginning of the recklessness of God.
God spoke directly into a new Word, articulated a more
    intimate word of love,
proclaimed Good news, declared God's self into the world.
    In the new beginning the God breathed, Word became
    clothed in flesh and blood, became the Word of life,
became the Word of love spoken anew. Spoken into the
    world. Spoken in and through human form.

And so it was the beginning of Him who created the
    beginning, coming into the world.
Of the light of the world appearing in vulnerable humanity.
    Of the Creator wrapped in swaddling bands and held in
    the loving arms of a mother.
Of the only Son—small, weak, and vulnerable—
entrusted to human caring,
to human fragility,
to human uncertainty,
to human obscurity.

It was the beginning of the God Word fleshed out in
    human form, exposed
to human doubt and faithlessness, to human falseness
    and hatred, to human abuse and deception.

It was the beginning of the image of the invisible God
    revealing human love and steadfastness, human
    dependability and trustworthiness, constancy and courage,
faithfulness and strength.

It was the beginning of the Word, spoken in flesh,
    coming into the world,
transforming those who listened, testifying to those who
    are hopeless and doubting,
enlightening those who walk in darkness, adopting those
    who are orphans.

Since the foundation of the world when God spoke
    the beginning words of love,
God has continued to speak openheartedly, will continue
    speaking unreservedly the word of love to us,
    recklessly risking everything to offer us the
    beginning of the future.

Elizabeth

The first few weeks were wonderful.
Can you imagine a husband who can't speak?
Can't tell you to stop nagging!
Can't tell you "NO!" when you invite your mother to stay!
Can't disagree with your assessment of the situation!
Can't offer an opinion when you decide that it really is time
    to replace the living room carpet!
Can't tell you it's too expensive!

But after a few weeks you realise he can't ask for directions
    while you drive
round and round the same bit of ring road trying to visit
    your sister.
Can't help you with the crossword clues.
Can't choose names for the baby.
Can't tell you he loves you.
I think that was the worst part. It shouldn't matter,
    should it? Actions speak louder than words. But not
    hearing him actually say he loved me for those nine
    long months,
was really hard.
We both new this baby was a gift from God.
I knew the moment I fell pregnant there was going to be
    something special about him.
Knew he was going to be a 'he'; funny, so did Zechariah.

Funny, isn't it, how you just know things sometimes?
I think that's when you hear God speak, when you just
    know something deep down inside yourself, as if
    somebody just whispered it in your ear.

We both knew he was going to be called "John"; and that
    was the first thing Zechariah said, at the end of those
    long nine months, "John – his name is John!"

Mary's Mother

I suppose the gold will be useful, and you could sell the
    frankincense and myrrh.
Now, Mary, before you say anything, what *possible* use will
    they be for a baby? . . .
You and Joseph are going to need a bit extra now you have
    a family to support.

She wouldn't hear of it though.
That was my Mary. . . .
When she made her mind up there was no moving her.
I don't know *where* she gets her wilfulness from.

I do know where she gets her ideas from though . . . her father!
Not a practical bone in his body! But plenty of nonsense
    about ancestors,
and about God, and about faithfulness!
It's all very well, I tell him, but you have been faithful,
    for years and years.
Look at us, still living in the same old house, with the same
    old stuff, doing the same old things; when is God going
    to favour us!?

I blame him for the whole thing! He fills her head with
    nonsense about the Messiah,
being born of David's line. She even told me once,
"Mum, what do you think? The Messiah is going to be born
    into our family;
what if you were God's Grandma?"
We laughed. . . .

And then she was expecting a baby, and Joseph swearing
    it wasn't his.
He was less than useless, too, wouldn't face up to his
    responsibilities,
left my poor Mary to shoulder it alone.

Those few months were terrible—all that talk about angels
    and God's baby!
Ohh, I could have rung her neck! AND her father's!!
    He wasn't much use:
"What if it's true?" he kept asking. "What if it's true?"

Would you have believed her? If she was your daughter?
Her whole life ahead of her, she believes she's having
    God's son!
It's just not what I wanted for her! It's not what any
    parent wants, is it?
To see their child turned into an adult overnight,
    shouldering all sorts of responsibilities they shouldn't
    have to think about yet . . .
and the taunts—the other children said some very cruel
    things, encouraged by their parents no doubt.

I sent her away to stay with a cousin, Elizabeth, in the end,
    just to give us all a break
from the endless bickering and worry.

When she came back, that Joseph was straight round here.
    I sent her father out to deal with him; I thought he'd
    come to cause trouble again . . .
Maybe I misjudged him, I don't know . . . but suddenly he
    was begging Mary's forgiveness and telling her that God
    had explained everything to him in a dream.
I wish someone would explain it to me. . . .

What a pair!
Both with their heads in the clouds!
Both seeing visions!
How they'll cope with a baby I've no idea!
AND if ANYBODY ELSE tells me that I'm going to be
    God's Grandma. . . .

A Neighbour

They knocked on my door first. I didn't answer.
I'd seen them, wandering up and down knocking on doors.

They looked as if they'd been on the road a long time . . .
He seemed very protective of her, always his arm tightly
    wrapped 'round her shoulder.
It wasn't till they got nearer that I realised why. Pregnant!
    And hardly more than a schoolgirl!

The main street was heaving. Goodness know, this census
    had turned the whole town upside down! People coming
    from all over, trying to find a bed for the night . . .
It was chaos . . .

And then the knock at the door and I knew it was them . . . ,
    but I didn't answer.
I was afraid. I didn't want to get involved . . . I didn't know
    them . . .
She seemed so tiny.

Later on that night I heard her having the baby,
    heard it crying.
And I felt glad that it was okay, and I felt sad that I hadn't
    offered them a helping hand . . .
But I didn't know them . . . they were strangers . . .

I looked out of the bedroom window into the next door
    garden, into the garage.
The lights were on inside and I could see her, that tiny
    little girl holding the baby.
He still stood with his arms around them both.
What a place to have a baby!

Angel Gabriel

I hope you weren't expecting the usual tinsel crown and
    white robe
you dress us up in, like pantomime characters!

I couldn't believe it when He told me . . .
I mean, I'd always known it was going to be a rough ride,
    but . . . Bethlehem!
In a stable!
In the middle of the night!
Alone?!
Madness!!
But then He's not one for doing things the easy way,
    not our God . . .
Always been a bit of a risk taker;
Well, you only have to look at you lot to see that!

And as a baby . . . ? No need for that either . . . that's what
    He has us for—
well us, and the prophets, and one or two others—Moses . . .

A baby!!!
Can you imagine the risk!!?? Two thousand years ago
    in a stable?
What was He thinking?

The Creator of the universe, this majestic, awesome God.
And He chooses to announce his arrival to a group of
    shepherds, some mystic sect,
and a grumpy old innkeeper and his wife!

Amazing—and so typical! Prepared to risk everything,
   even life itself,
to speak to you . . .

Sometimes our God is a complete mystery to me . . .
   Well, I guess you know all about that!

.... ℘

Shepherd's wife

I've never seen anything like it!
Blackpool illuminations it was!
The whole sky bright and shining!
It must have been visible for miles!

I wouldn't have believed it if I hadn't seen it myself.
Thomas came running back from the fields, shouting at the
    top of his voice.
I wondered what on earth was going on.
I just got in the bath for goodness sake!

"June," he shouted, "June, come and see this. Come on,
    woman!!
You're going to miss it all!"

Well, it's not like my Thomas to make a fuss over something,
in fact, not like Thomas to make a fuss over anything!!
I jumped out of the bath, as hastily and elegantly as age
    would allow,
threw on my dressing gown; all the time he's shouting
    like a madman
from outside the house, "Come on, woman—what are you
    playing at!?"

When I got to the front door, I could hardly believe
    my eyes . . .
the sky was full of light, swirling rainbow coloured light,
    and the music!

At first, such a simple, single, beautiful sound and then
    building and building.
There were no words. I'm sure there were no words,
    but it was as if the music itself could speak straight
    into your heart.

And we knew we had to go, we had to find out,
    we had to see for ourselves . . .

Passerby

There were lights on in the stable when I passed.
There was light on the outside, too—the whole place bathed
     in gentle light . . .
Beautiful . . .
That's what caught my attention—the beautiful light.
I wasn't going to go in;
I mean it would only be full of animals anyway . . . and then
     I heard a cry,
a baby cry, small, but strong, demanding! Must be hungry!
A stable is no place for a baby!

Another cry and the sound of hushed voices. Well, it's not
     my business,
I should just get home, Hannah will worry . . .

But that light was so warm and so . . . light! Well, just a
     quick peep,
to make sure everything's alright, and then I'll be on
     my way . . .

Moving nearer to the door, peering into the stable, I see
     inside a man and a young woman, in her arms a bundle
     of cloth, the baby I assumed . . .
She was singing softly and gently rocking it on her knee.
The man was trying to get a fire going in a brazier.

She said something to him, the man bent over the bundle
     smiling; and then she smiled up at him.

I felt awkward. This was a private moment, not meant
     for me to see.
Quietly I slipped away.

Dunno what happened to them, but something important
    had happened!
that night . . .
in a stable . . .
in Bethlehem town . . .

Bethlehem.

My walls tremble with grief!
My foundations shake with anger!
How could they do this?
What were they thinking?

Soldiers beat down the doors,
wrenched the boys out of their arms—
only a few years old,
hardly even begun to live,
and now they're dead
at the point of a Roman sword.

My streets and buildings have housed these strangers.
My waters and fields have fed them.
And in return they murder my children!
Don't they have children of their own?
Can they not hear the weeping in my streets,
the sorrow running in rivers down my paths?
My stone heart is broken
and I will never recover,
never understand this senseless slaughter!

Though my buildings stand,
and my highways and thoroughfares remain open,
I am broken!
I am pierced by the cries of my daughters!
Inconsolable,
as they mourn the death of their little ones!

Nothing

Once there was nothing,
  and God breathed into it
  and made darkness and light.
The light shone in the darkness,
  bringing light to all people.
And it was good.
And people lived in the light,
in peace,
in hope,
in truth.

And the darkness brought evening and rest, a chance
  to imagine,
and to dream, for visions and revelation, and it was also good.

But some discovered darkness can be used to frighten!
That the shadows are a good place to hide!
  That in the darkness things can be
  forgotten!
That darkness can be used—to conceal
  the malevolence
  in human hearts,
to obscure the truth, to blot out the light!
And so some people learned to love the
  darkness! And the darkness seemed
  to overcome the light! And so the
  people walked in darkness, and
  waited in darkness,
and the darkness was exploited and used
  to bring hunger and pain!
Struggle and heartache!
Disease and anger!
Violence and war!
Using the darkness of human souls, striking at the vulnerable
  and the weak,

turning the hearts of ordinary people to acts of unimaginable
    violence and neglect.

And so a shroud of darkness covers the earth—This not the
    darkness as it was meant to be, made by God,
a time for rest and peace,
to think and to imagine,
darkness full of possibility.
This is deep darkness, great and terrible, full of pain and hurt,
    feeding on greed and selfishness.
Until . . . the time when the light would return.

But in the deep darkness God's light still shone
in those who wait in hope, who trust that the light
    will return.

And so many years have passed, and in the dark a teenage girl
    is visited by the light.
And in the darkness of her womb God's light is growing.
Mary rejoices that God's light is returning to the world,
    but her fiancé loses faith, calls off the wedding.

Nevertheless, the light is coming!
   And so, in the darkness
   of a dream, Joseph is
   encouraged and his faith
   is restored.

In the deep darkness a self-
   declared king calls a census
   on a whim.
A heavily pregnant, unmarried
   mother, who hasn't thought
   to book in advance,
arrives in an unfamiliar city with her partner, looking for
   accommodation.
Unsurprisingly everywhere is already booked up!
It looks like they will have to spend the night sleeping
   on the streets.
But the light is coming!

And in the deep darkness a harried and impatient hotel
   manager
has no time to spend on people who cannot organise
   themselves,
especially people like them—no money, not even married!
How would he survive in business if he didn't plan ahead?
"It's not my problem," he mutters, as he indicates to the
   porter to move them on.

And in the darkness of the night the woman moans
   in pain!
This baby won't wait for a comfy hospitable bed.
Because the light is coming!

And a kindly old man with no room to offer, proposes a bed
   in a stable,
warm and dry. He offers food and blankets.

And in the deep darkness, the king of the universe
    is born, amongst dirty hay and smelly animals;
    and because it's dark, the baby is laid in an
    animal food stall.
No nurse or doctor present, no celebration or family event.
But now the light is here!

And in the darkness of the night, a group of shepherds
    huddle round
a small fire for warmth, watching the sheep on a hillside.
    Nobody notices them;
they could freeze out there on the hills.
But the light is here!

And suddenly the darkness of the night sky is filled
    with light!
And God sings of the light coming into the world!
And the shepherds filled with light and hope and joy,
    follow the song, to the stable in Bethlehem.

But in the deep darkness a selfish and anxious king,
    fearing rumours that the light had come, that a king
    would rise, searches for the light to destroy it.
But the light has come!

And faraway some stargazers see a new light in the sky
    and set off to discover the source.

And in the deep darkness a baby cries!
Announces his arrival!
Declares the light has come into the world!
Proclaims that God himself has become the light for
    all people!
The baby born in darkness is the light of God!
And the light blazes in the darkness over a stable in
    Bethlehem!

And many will ask how can the light of God be born
into human weakness,
human suffering,
into a tiny human baby?

And as the baby grows many will seek to extinguish
    the light He brings, restoring sight to the blind,
    bringing freedom to the captive
proclaiming God's light and love to all who will listen.

But there are still those who choose to use and abuse the
    deep darkness that has grown within the human spirit.

And so a young man, with nothing much to recommend him,
    except the testimony of a few followers, is pronounced
    guilty without trial and declared a criminal.
Stripped and beaten, he is dragged out onto a hillside and put
    to death and buried in a borrowed grave, because there
    are those who prefer the deep darkness.

But in the morning God's light blazes in an empty tomb!
And the deep darkness roars in anger because it can never
    win, even when it seems as if God's light has gone out,
    and people choose deep darkness.

And so a mother and baby lie starving by the side of the road.
A young boy is given a gun and forced to fight!
A young woman comforts her father as he weeps over the
    torn and mutilated
body of his wife!
But God's light will not be put out!

God knows that only the one who made the darkness
for rest and peace,
for dreams and visions,
for imagination and possibility
can re-embrace it!

Can redeem it!
Can reclaim it!
Can teach us how to use it well!

And so, in the deep and pain-ridden darkness, God's light
   is being reborn, and in that birth transforming the deep
   darkness,
chasing away the shadows, bringing peace and love and rest,
   giving us freedom from
the fear of darkness and a chance to embrace the light.

After the accident

The morning after the night before

It see-e-e-e-eps into joints
and,
through the day, plagues
each action with its inces-s- ant
gnawing.
At each moment an effort
beyond belief
is called for . . .
At night it sleeps

leaving room
only for thought,
no rest,
only dreaming,
endless flickering of
the SAME film.
Till . . .
dawn breaks, and in, it cree- ee – ee- eeps
and settles like a heavy coat
over the day,
over me!
Overcoat of lethargy. NO!
More than that!
Of bone-aching tiredness!

Working it out

As I sit and think,
I write.
Small scrawls.
Smudges.
Squiggles.
Which once made sense of the world.
Now they are random,
chaotic.
I cannot understand them!
How can I see the picture
when there is no frame
of reference?
Only marks on paper
refusing to be words.

Wishing it were different

Wishing it were different—what?
That these things had not
come to pass?
Shall not pass for life?
Where is laughter?
Overtaken by pain,
or simply the effort of getting through the day?
Is this really living?
Only visible the monochrome world,
nothing glows, or grows, or delights.
Everything is dull!
Why do I mourn the loss of that which is not mine,
was never mine to lose?

How?

How do people cope
when it feels as if their
world has ended?
Where do they go for comfort
when what stands between them
feels too wide to cross,
too hard to break,
too difficult to articulate?
Where do they go to express themselves,
how do they learn to speak again,
in a new language?
How to trust the words have meaning,
can express the inexpressible?
I want to know how to talk again,
in words which can contain my pain!

How II?

How can it be gone?
Where is it now—
that part of you,
which I no longer
see?
Thrown out in some plastic bag?
Burned like so much rubbish?
Your poor butchered flesh, which
I washed and held,
encouraged to take its first
s
    tep
        s,
bathed the knee,
wrapped the ankle,
bought new shoes?
How can it not be there now?

Moments

There are moments when for
just a moment,
these moments never came to pass.
I can feel the moment
of you lying in the road,
the moment I have so feared,
the moment which will
change everything.
Or that moment
when I saw the wounds gaping!
Moments of pain!
Moments of horror!
Moment! A moment!
What a ridiculous name for
the seconds which drive our
lives into completely new
directions!
A moment is both a blessing and a curse
or just a curse!
Lived a moment, lived a lifetime!
Moment . . . now . . . here . . . back then?
IT NEVER HAPPENED!!
I imagine other moments
never to pass now.

The journey

Journeys are the
in-between places of our lives,
places where we can be ourselves.
Places where we don't
have to know
the answer,
only begin
to formulate
the question.
The more we live
the more we learn to like
"between."

Talk

All this talk of God is fine,
but what does He actually do?
I'm told that the world is
in a delicate state of balance.
So does He sit in heaven balancing it all
like some omniscient set of scales?

All this talking to God is fine,
but when is he going to answer?
If praying changes the world,
then why is it still such a mess?
Has the number of calls overwhelmed
the omnipresent telephone exchange?

All this listening to God is fine,
but when will He actually speak?
Plenty of those who appear to hear him
don't seem to understand what He said.

Lent

Wilderness I

Cold.
Freezing.
Bitter.
Icy.
No solid rock,
just sinking sand.

Faithfulness fled!
Mercy turned masochist!
Compassion now coldness!
Justice a joke!
No solid ground,
just shifting sand.
Tears.
Pain.
Hurt.
Anger.
No solid ground,
just shifting sand.

Ask and you will be denied!
Seek and you shall be lost!
Knock and your knuckles will be raw!
Give and you will have nothing left!
No solid ground,
just shifting sand.

Alone.
Silence.
Lost.
Weary.
No solid ground,
just shifting sand.

Wilderness II

Still
sinking.
Still
struggling.

Where are You?
I'm still sinking.

Where are You?
I'm still struggling.
Where are You?
Didn't You come here first?
Forty days and nights—
a holiday!
I've spent most of my life here!
In the wilderness,
sinking.
Pretending that I can walk on sand,
making it appear like solid ground.
Clever, eh?!

Where are You?
I will be with you always . . . *!#?
Except here
in the desert,
in the sinking
sand.

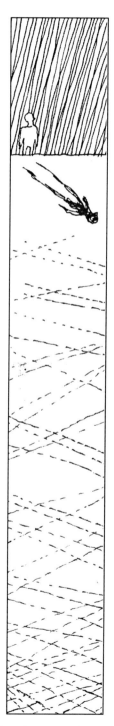

Wilderness III

I'm still here
And You are . . .
not!
Or is it more that You enjoy
some cosmic game of hide and seek?
Coming, ready or not!
Where can I flee from Your presence?
Well, HERE, apparently.

Wilderness IV

How long do You think
we can keep this up,
this one-sided conversation?

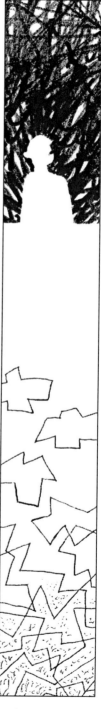

Wilderness V

I would so like
this journey to have a happy ending.
A blinding light perhaps?
A vision of heaven?
A sense of warmth
or peace perhaps?
A few cooing doves?
And maybe a song,
with lots of clapping,
and a happy tune?
A shout of joy?
An empty tomb?
Right now I'll settle for a map
And a drink of water.

Wilderness VI

Inside, the sand heaves and moans
like some groaning bellyache.
And I sink deeper . . .
Why dost thou torment us thus?
(Note the polite use of biblical
      language.)
I've heard it said that
God's a BASTARD!
Are You?

You were *driven* into the wilderness,
compelled by God to endure
the solitude,
the fear,
the cold,
the sinking sand.
Do You hate your Father too?

Wilderness VII

Cannot even retrace my footsteps.
Sand shifts.
Footprints disappear.
Footprints!!
"It was then that I carried you."
Oh, really!
Seems to me,
at the most difficult times in my life,
when there was only one set of
    footprints in the sand,
it was then that you abandoned me.

Wilderness VIII

If You know what it is like
to be lost,
alone,
friendless,
hopeless
and if You come to show the way,
then why
am I still out here drowning
    in the sand?

Wilderness IX

When you were in the desert,
angels came and waited on you.
When you were in the desert,
you were taken by someone you knew.

So how does it work for the rest of us,
who find ourselves out here alone?
Where are our angel waiters
or the friend to see us home?

Wilderness X

When You were *compelled* to be here,
driven away from all You knew,
did You ever rage at heaven?
Did You ever question why?
Did You ever wish you'd never come?
Because if You did, maybe I can too?

And when you wandered tired
   and weary,
sand shifting under you feet,
did you ever feel like giving up?
Did you ever think about going home?
Did you ever wholly lose your way?
Because if you did, then can I too?

And when it was dark and the
   coldness came,
while you shivered and wept alone,
did you know yourself loved?
Did you open your heart?
Did you still follow the call?
Because if you did, then I might too?

Because if you did,
and if I can too,
perhaps I could take your hand?
Because if you did,
and if I can too,
perhaps I could stay with you?
Because if you did
and I can too,
perhaps you will take me home?

Easter

The man who went to bury his father

I wish He hadn't said it.
I tried so hard to avoid His gaze and the inevitable invitation,
"Follow me."
I knew what He was going to say before the words
    left His lips.
I'd already turned away, but *knew* He was talking to me.
I knew I should have kept on walking, and then I could
    have told myself
He didn't mean *me*; but there was something in that voice
    that you couldn't ignore.

The trouble was He just didn't understand—not everybody
    can just drop their responsibilities, just like that. If we all
    just left everything, the world would be a right old mess.

The world needs people like me, the ones who stay put and
    stick it out regardless!

"Follow me." The words still echoed in my head. I could
    feel myself turning back towards Him. "I have other
    commitments," I muttered—"my family."
And for a moment we looked at each other; His piercing eyes
    searched my soul,
and I knew He knew my fear.
Fear of being wrong,
of what others would think,
of letting Him down.

So I turned away. When I looked back, He'd gone, pushed on
    by the crowd.
I'd lost the moment forever!
I wanted to run after Him; Instead, I turned towards home,
safety,
routine,
the things I was good at, the things I knew.

Afterwards, when I heard the things He'd said and done,
    I wished I'd had the courage to find Him, tell Him
    I was wrong, that I was ready now . . .
Then I heard He had been killed. It's too late now.

But I never forgot that time. The time He offered me
    adventure,
the day that could have made a difference, but I was
    too afraid to let go.

Martha

I had hoped He would come sooner.
Since He had become more popular, He spent more and more
    time away from home.
He and Lazarus had been friends for years. They loved each
    other like brothers.
When my brother fell ill, I felt sure He would come.
But He didn't.

And when we knew it was terminal, we left messages in all
    the usual places,
hoping that He would get one and come back to see my
    brother before he died,
but He didn't.

My brother had been dead for four days before He
    finally came,
with a whole troop of hangers on, people we didn't
    even know,
who seemed to think they had a perfect right to be here and
    trample all over our grief.
As if we didn't have enough to do making the arrangements,
without having to entertain them!

Finally, the day after He arrived, I couldn't stand it any longer.
I was angry!
So angry!
That He hadn't made the effort to come when He knew my
    brother was dying.
Angry that He had brought all those people when we just
    wanted a quiet little funeral.
Family and close friends only!
Angry that He didn't seem upset!
And I was angry at the world, which could allow such a
    beautiful, talented brother

to die so young, before he had really lived! I hate death!—It's
    so unfair!

He came into the kitchen where I was, still washing up the
    endless stream
of coffee mugs that *His* hangers on had been using that day,
    and my anger just poured out!

"He only wanted to see *you* before he died. He kept asking
    for *you*!
We sent messages, but *you* never came! Why didn't
    you come!
Are *you* such a big celebrity now that we're beneath *your*
    time and attention!
I suppose now *you* have all those followers *you* don't need us
    any more!"
I was so angry! Angry because He didn't come, because He
    brought all those people!
BECAUSE! . . . because . . .

Because . . . I wished that I had spent more time with my
    brother before he died . . .
I couldn't bear to look at him, to see him suffering like that,
    so I kept myself busy,
bringing food,
cleaning the house,
tidying his things,
getting whatever he needed,
anything to take my mind off the fact that he was dying.
And now he is gone I wish more than anything I had spent
    more time simply being with him. I wish I hadn't been so
    afraid to tell him all the things I wanted to.
I feel cheated, cheated that I didn't allow myself to say
    goodbye properly,
to take my time with him.
I miss him so much.

And so we went to visit my brother.

I don't understand these people who say that the dead look
    peaceful;
to me they just look all wrong. People are not meant to be
    so still,
so . . . lifeless. Those we love are wrenched away from us;
    we are left with emptiness
which can never be filled.

And of course the rest of them followed us, crowding outside
    the tomb.
Jesus stood outside and cried, big tears running down His
    cheeks.
Stretching out His hands He spoke, "Father, please restore the
    life of my friend,
that they will know I am your son."
It was a sad prayer, the prayer of someone who wished he
    had been able to say goodbye properly.

But then the crowd grew quiet, deathly quiet, and there was
    a strange kind of warmth
and then a sound, like someone drawing in a deep breath.
Jesus stretched out His hand and grasped my brother's
    hand; and as He did so, my brother began to sit up, tears
    streaming down his face.
Someone near the front fainted; another woman screamed
    in panic!
As He reached forward, they greeted one another
    like long lost friends.

Whatever happened to Lazarus?

Whatever happened to Lazarus
once he was brought back to life?
What did he do with the bandages
that wrapped him from head to foot?
What did he eat that evening
as he pondered the meaning of life?
Where did he go the day after—
back to the scene of the crime?
Did anyone ever ask him
if he wanted another chance?
How did he go on living
knowing he was already dead?

Discipleship

When the disciples went home to say good-bye to their
    families and tell them all that
Jesus was sending them out, there was uproar!!

Matthew's Dad said, "You're going where? For how long?
    Taking *nothing* with you?
I think I' d better have a word Him."

Peter's Mother said, "But what about these marmite
    sandwiches?"
"He said no bread, mam," said Peter. His mum got that funny
    glint in her eye.
"He didn't say cake though did He—or apples ?"

It wasn't any better in Mark's house: "Nothing on your feet!?"
    his mum shouted;

1 "How many times have I told you not to walk around with
2   nothing on your *feet*!
3 We'll just see about that!"
4
5 When James and John told their Dad, he went out and
6   bought new camping rucksacks.
7 Bartholomew's Dad insisted he bring some money.
8
9 So the following morning, when the disciples gathered
10   'round Jesus,
11 Matthew's dad came to have a word with Him,
12 Peter came dragging a big hamper of food,
13 Mark came in his nice new trainers, carrying his wellies,
14 James and John came with bulging rucksacks,
15 and Bartholomew came with a wallet full of money.
16
17 Jesus looked at them and sighed.
18 "Why do you think I told you not to bring bread?"
19 "No bread in here!" said Peter, throwing back the lid of the
20   hamper,
21 "You can check if you like."
22
23 Jesus turned to Mark: "And you?"
24 "You just said no sandals, and I'm not wearing any!"
25
26 Jesus looked at James and John, with their bulging rucksacks.
27 "Let me guess," said Jesus; "those aren't really bags;
28   they're rucksacks."
29 "Got it in one!" grinned James and John together.
30
31 "It's not a purse; it's a wallet," mumbled Bartholomew,
32   as he caught Jesus' eye.
33
34 "What's the most important thing you need to do on this
35   journey?" asked Jesus.
36 "Make sure we eat properly," said Peter.
37

"Wear the correct shoes," said Mark, "and *mine* are nice
  new ones!"
"Stay dry and warm!" said James and John, together.
"Keep your money in a safe place," said Bartholomew.
"And while you are worrying about all of that,"
  said Jesus,
"whose going to tell the people that God loves them?"

Pentecost

It was the time for waiting.
The in-between time.
The wilderness time.
It was the "we didn't know what to do next" time.

In the before time, Jesus had been with us again.
Had talked with us, eaten with us, even caught fish with us.

But then He went again and afterwards we were left,
    wondering . . .
Amazed, but wondering.
A little confused and wondering . . .
Wondering and speculating.

What would be next? Speculating and remembering.

The life we had spent with Him had been Wonderful!
Scary!
Amazing!
Difficult!
Astonishing!
Complicated!
Miraculous!
Demanding!
Extraordinary!
Desperate!
Death defying!
But what next . . . ?
It was the "what do we do now" time,
"how do we tell what God has done" time,
"how to put it into words" time,
the "what to say now" time.

So we did what we had always tried to do: follow
    His instructions.

"Wait in Jerusalem . . . and I will send the Holy Spirit,
    just as my Father promised."

So we waited, in a house, in the heat, in the dry thirstiness
    of the day;
we waited . . . And we wondered, as we always did,
    about Jesus, about the prophecies;
and we speculated and remembered what they said about
    the Spirit of God:

"I have put my spirit on Him. He will bring justice to the
    nations."
Was that the spirit we were waiting for? The Bringer of
    Justice?

We wondered about Jesus, about the first passage of scripture
we ever heard Him read:

"The Spirit of the lord is upon me, for the Lord has
    anointed me
to bring good news to the poor, comfort to the
    brokenhearted,
release to the captives, to proclaim the year of the Lord's
    favour."

A dynamic spirit,
anointing,
comforting,
releasing and proclaiming.

Was this who we were waiting for in the heat of the day?
Wondering what would happen next?
Wondering and remembering?

Remembering some of the last conversations before Jesus
    died.

"I will ask and the Father will send you another advocate,
     the Holy Spirit.
The world does not know Him, but you know Him because
     He lives with you now
and will live within you."

And we wondered about the Spirit.
Advocate.
Supporter.
Activist.
Encourager.

It was so hot while we waited! The heat drained the life out
     of you!
Gradually the room became silent, and all of us were feeling
     the oppression of the heat,
and waiting, all of us, young and old, women and men,
waiting and remembering.

"In those days I will pour out my Spirit on all peoples.
Your sons and daughters will prophesy.
Your young men will see visions.
In those days I will pour out my Spirit
even on my servants—men and women alike . . ."

Was this the day we were waiting for? In the heat?
And the dryness? And the silence that added to the
     apprehension,
and the feeling of oppression, and the loss of speech, and of
     purpose?

And in the quiet, a whisper of air began to drift.
And we began to stir.

And the air around us began to stir, as if new life had been
     breathed.

The air was cool and refreshing, bringing the beginning of life
    and energy,
bringing a sense of expectancy.

Moving now with strength and purpose, it became louder,
    no longer a whisper,
but the very air shouting around us!

And we began to speak too— first a whisper, as if we were
    learning how to speak,
to articulate,
to communicate;
as if the air was teaching us how to speak for the very
    first time.
And then it was gone,
as if a whirlwind had rushed through the room, bringing
    energy and excitement,
as if waking us from sleep.

And after the wind came the fire, brightly coloured, dancing
    over our heads,
filled with colour and vitality, gently caressing our heads
    and faces,
releasing us from the lethargy of the heat.

And we began to talk louder, louder with excitement and
    energy,
as if we had been shown a whole new world.
And we shared with one another, and with those around us,
    how wonderful,
how marvellous God was, and is and is becoming, in us,
here, today!

The words just came, poured out, different words speaking
    to different people,
about their experiences of God, speaking God into the lives
    of those willing to hear;

and yet, within that diversity, within that difference,
a sense of common purpose, a sense of identity,

as if the different words were forming harmonies,
    and as the harmonies came together
so the picture of God became richer.

More dynamic!
More vigorous!
More vibrant!
More Godlike! . . .

As if God was breaking out, leaping through the jumble
    of words,
proclaiming Himself here and now, through the richness
    and variety of the voices.

Wild.
Unreserved.
Unrestrained Love!
The completeness of God's giving now living within us
    and in all who call upon His name.

Provoking questions.
Refreshing spirits.
Encouraging speech.
Bringing purpose.
And most of all proclaiming the Good News of God
in all who call upon His name, to all who have not
    yet heard . . .

Lightning Source UK Ltd.
Milton Keynes UK
13 March 2010

151340UK00001B/14/P